Makeup Magic
Your Transformative Handbook

BY LIGIA CENTENO

This book is dedicated to all the everyday women who strive to enhance their natural beauty and confidence. Your individuality inspires this journey. Here's to embracing your unique charm and feeling beautiful every day.

Table of Content

CHAPTER 1:
The Foundation (Pun Intended!)

Hey there, fabulous face! Ready to dive into the world of skin basics before slathering on that makeup magic? Let's start by getting to know your skin because, well, it's kind of a big deal! Your skin isn't just there for looks; it's a dynamic canvas that changes with the weather, age, what you munch on, and how you're feeling health-wise. So, picking the right makeup pals for your skin type is like choosing the right squad for a road trip—essential!

Skin Types 101:

Alright, picture this: your skin can be as chill as a cucumber (normal), a combo of oily and dry (combo), as oily as a pizza slice (oily), or maybe as dry as the Sahara (dry). Knowing your type helps you find the perfect products that'll have your skin saying, "Oh yeah, that's the good stuff!"

What's your skin type? Are you more of a "chill cucumber," "combo queen," "pizza slice oily," or "Sahara desert dry"? Write it down and jot down three makeup products that would suit your skin type.

Skin Care Safari:

Do you have a skin routine? It's like a dance party for your face, keeping that glow game strong and making makeup go on like butter. Speaking of parties, don't let excess facial hair crash this one! Keep those brows in check, say adios to peach fuzz, and send chin hairs packing.

Describe your current skin routine. Is it a full-on dance party or more of a quick two-step? Write down one new thing you'll add to your routine to pamper your skin.

Prepping Your Canvas:

Clean slate, baby! Before you slap on any makeup, your skin needs to be as clean as a whistle. A spritz of hydrating mist or a dash of setting spray will give your skin extra hydration and will make blending easier. The proper setting spray will give you a layer of soft hold that will give your makeup lasting power. You can spray between layers and after you have finished your makeup. Oh, and when you're massaging in that moisturizer, think of it as giving your face a mini spa vacation.

What's your go-to method for cleaning your face before makeup? Do you prefer a hydrating mist or a setting spray? Write down your choice and explain why you like it.

Pro Tip Alert! Adjust your moisturizer depending on the condition of your skin. As the seasons change, your skin may need less or more emollient products depending on the weather. You may also have to change your moisturizer due to hormonal or changes to skin due to age. Your skin will thank you later!

Weather check! Is it hot like summer or chilly like winter where you live? Pick the right moisturizer for the season and tell us why it's perfect for your skin.

Primers, Primers, Baby:

To prime or not to prime? That is the question. Even though primers are optional, think of them as your makeup wingmen, helping with oil control or keeping that glam on lock all day. But remember, don't go overboard. Your skin's gotta breathe too!

To prime or not to prime? That is the question! Do you feel like your skin needs a primer buddy? Write down one reason why you might use a primer, or if you're all about that natural glow, tell us why you're skipping it.

Makeup Mixer:
The Order of Operations:

No rulebook here, but if you're new to this makeup party, following a few steps can be a lifesaver. First up, the foundation—aka the MVP of your makeup routine. It's like a flawless filter for your face, smoothing things out and getting you ready for the main event.

Let's talk foundation! Which type of coverage speaks to your soul: light and breezy, full-on glam, or buildable babe? Circle your fave and explain how it matches your makeup style.

Foundation Finish Fiesta: Your Guide to Flawless Faces

Alright, gorgeous, let's talk foundation finishes! Think of it like choosing the perfect outfit for your skin—there's a style for every occasion. Here's the lowdown on finding your flawless finish:

1.Sheer Coverage	• **Description:** Think of it as your skin's BFF—sheer coverage lets your natural beauty shine through while giving you a little boost. • **Effect:** It's like your skin, but better! Smooths things out without hiding your freckles or that cute little mole. • **Finish:** Hello, glow! It's all about that fresh, dewy look that says, "I woke up like this." • **Ideal for:** Those days when you want to feel light, breezy, and effortlessly beautiful.
2.Light to Medium Coverage	• **Description:** It's like your skin's favorite cozy sweater—comfortable, familiar, and just the right amount of coverage. • **Effect:** Smooths things over without stealing the show. It's like your skin's secret admirer, giving it a little boost of confidence. • **Finish:** Radiant and natural, with a hint of "I'm ready to take on the world" glow. • **Ideal for:** Everyday adventures, from brunch with pals to conquering that big presentation at work.

3.Buildable Coverage	- **Description:** Think of it as your skin's chameleon—able to adapt to any situation with a quick layer or two. - **Effect:** Want a sheer look for running errands? No prob. Need full-on glam for a night out? Just layer it up, babe! - **Finish:** Versatility is the name of the game here—whether you're feeling low-key or ready to slay, this foundation's got your back. - **Ideal for:** Those who love to switch things up and embrace their inner makeup artist.
4.Full Coverage	- **Description:** Meet your skin's superhero—full coverage swoops in to save the day, concealing everything from blemishes to bad days. - **Effect:** Flawless. Absolutely flawless. It's like hitting the reset button on your skin, erasing imperfections like they were never there. - **Finish:** Smooth, polished, and oh-so-perfect. This foundation means business, honey! - **Ideal for:** When you need to bring your A-game, whether it's a hot date or a big event where you want to steal the spotlight.

So, there you have it, makeup mavens! Whether you're all about that barely-there beauty or you're ready to slay with full-on glam, there's a foundation finish out there with your name on it. Get ready to rock that flawless face and conquer the world—one fabulous finish at a time!

Let's talk foundation!

Which type of coverage speaks to your soul:

- light and breezy
- full-on glam
- buildable babe?

Circle your fave and explain how it matches your makeup style.

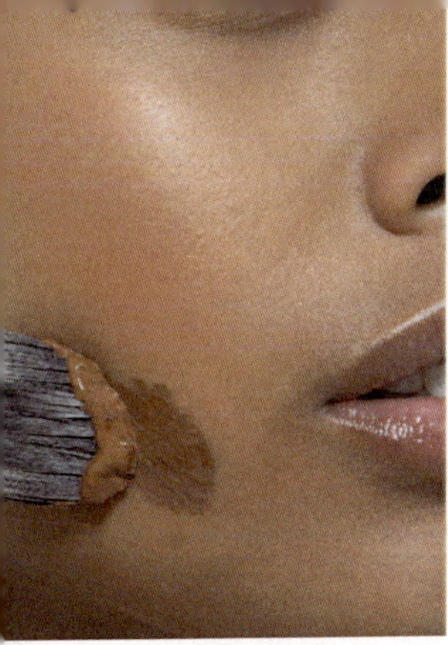

Tools of the Trade: Foundation Edition

Get ready to blend, buff, and beautify because we're diving deep into the world of foundation tools! Whether you're a beauty blender babe, a brush boss, or you prefer something totally different, there's a tool out there to make your foundation dreams come true. So, let's explore a variety of options and find the perfect match for your flawless face!

1.Beauty Blenders	• **Description:** These colorful sponges are like little miracle workers, giving you buildable coverage with a bounce. • **Dabbing:** Just dab, dab, dab away for a seamless finish that looks like second skin. • **Best for:** Those who love a soft, diffused look with just the right amount of coverage.
2.Full Head Brush	• **Description:** This brush means business, honey! With its dense bristles, it's all about maximum coverage with minimum effort. • **Stippling, Tapping Motion:** Tap, tap, tap your way to perfection for a flawless, airbrushed look that lasts all day. • **Best for:** When you need to cover up those pesky imperfections and slay all day and night.

3.Paddle Shaped Brush	• **Description:** With its flat, paddle-like shape, this brush is all about delivering light to medium coverage with ease. • **Sweeping, Patting Motion:** Sweep it on and pat it in for a soft, natural finish that's oh-so-flawless. • **Best for:** Those who want a subtle, everyday look that's as easy as swipe and go.
4.Fluffy Brush	• **Description:** Fluffy like a cloud, this brush is perfect for those who prefer a light touch. • **Circular, Sweeping Motion:** Swirl it on in gentle circles for a soft, diffused look that's sheer perfection. • **Best for:** When you want just a hint of coverage for that "barely there" beauty vibe.
5.Silicone Sponge	• **Description:** Smooth, sleek, and oh-so-satisfying to use, silicone sponges are like the futuristic version of traditional makeup tools. • **Swipe and Blend:** Glide it across your skin for a seamless application that's as smooth as silk. • **Best for:** Those who love a mess-free application and want to conserve product.

Flat-Top Kabuki Brush	- **Description:** This brush means business, with its flat top and dense bristles for a flawless finish. - **Buffing Motion:** Buff, buff, buff in small circles for a perfectly blended look that's selfie-ready. - **Best for:** When you need to achieve that airbrushed effect in seconds flat.
Dual-Ended Brush	- Description: Double the trouble, double the fun! This brush has two ends for ultimate versatility. - Precision Application: Use the smaller end for targeted coverage and the larger end for blending it all together seamlessly. - Best for: Those who want options—because why choose when you can have it all?
Fingers	- Description: Don't underestimate the power of your digits! Your fingers can be some of the most effective tools in your beauty arsenal. - Pat and Press: Warm up your foundation between your fingers and gently pat and press it into your skin for a natural, skin-like finish. - Best for: When you're on the go and need a quick touch-up, or when you just want to feel connected to your makeup routine.

So, whether you're swiping with silicone, buffing with a kabuki brush, or getting up close and personal with your fingertips, there's a tool out there that's perfect for you. Experiment, have fun, and get ready to slay that flawless face like never before!

Concealer Confessions:

Dark circles? Blemishes? No problemo! Concealer swoops in like a superhero to save the day. Pro tip: Triangles under the eyes are the secret weapon! Do not apply past the nose area.

Tip1:

If you do not have dark circles, purchase a concealer that is very close to your foundation shade. If you want to illuminate, choose a concealer one or two shades lighter than your skin tone..

Tip2:

If you have under eye circles, apply a color corrector first. Then, apply the concealer.

Dark circles be gone! How do you apply your concealer? Write down where you apply it, and share any tips or tricks you've picked up.

Lock it in, Baby!

After all that hard work, make sure your masterpiece stays put. Apply a little powder loose powder under the eyes to seal the concealer; apply a finishing powder on the rest of the face using a medium to large brush, and voilà! Your makeup is ready to slay all day.

> **Tip:**
> Seal the deal! After applying foundation and concealer, what's your finishing touch? Do you go for loose powder or skip it? Write down why you choose this step.

NOTES

NOTES

CHAPTER 2:
Adding Dimension to Your Face

Hey, gorgeous! Ready to add some oomph to that face of yours? We're diving into the world of contouring, eyeshadows, brows that slay, and cheeks that pop! But hey, don't worry, we're keeping it fun, easy, and totally relatable. Let's get started!

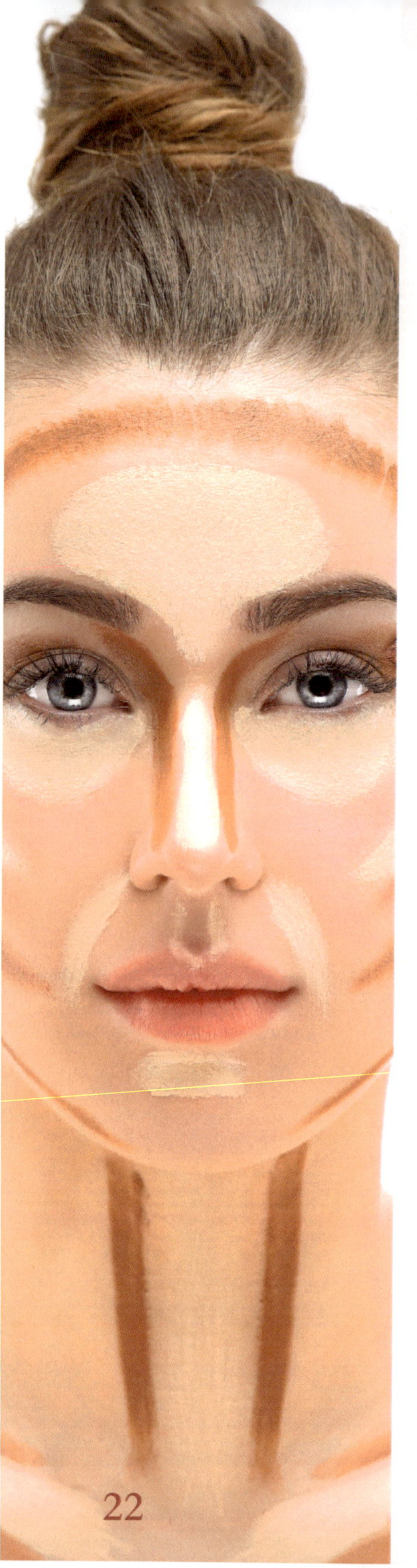

Contouring Chronicles:

So, contouring? It's like art for your face! We use light and dark shades to sculpt those cheekbones, define that jawline, and basically create magic. After foundation, things can get a bit flat, so let's bring back that 3D vibe!

Contouring Quest:

Contouring is like art for your face! What's your go-to contour technique: Soft and subtle or bold and chiseled? Write down which areas of your face you'd like to accentuate or minimize.

Easy Peasy Dimension: Soft Contour:

Want a simple everyday look that's still chef's kiss? After dusting finishing powder all over your face, grab your fave bronzer. Sweep it along the edges of your face, like on your forehead near the hairline and under those cheekbones. Voila! Instant definition!

Soft Contouring: Easy Peasy Dimension

Ready for that everyday glow-up? After setting powder, how do you apply your bronzer for that soft contour look? Describe the brush strokes or techniques you'd use.

Next-Level Sculpting: Cream Contour

Feeling a bit bold? Enter cream contour! Perfect for that "I woke up like this" vibe. Swipe it under those cheekbones, along your jawline, and around the edges of your face. Then, blend like your life depends on it!

Next-Level Sculpting: Cream Contour Craze

Feeling daring? Describe where you'd apply your cream contour for that "hello, cheekbones!" effect. How do you blend it seamlessly into your skin?

Let's Highlight Those Features:

Now, onto the glow-up! Highlighter is like fairy dust for your face. Dab it on the high points: cheekbones, nose tip, chin, or even the bridge of your nose. Get ready to shine bright like a diamond!

Highlighter Heaven:

Time to shine bright! Where do you place your highlighter to give your face that radiant glow? Name at least three areas you'd highlight.

Eyes That Mesmerize:

Let's talk eyes, babe! For an easy peasy look, grab two eyeshadows—one close to your skin tone and another for a pop of color. Swipe that light shade on your lids, then use a windshield wiper motion to blend the transition color in the crease. Think of it as creating a dreamy sunset on your eyes!

Give your eyes some definition! After you have finished the eyeshadow application, grab a pencil eyeliner, and draw a thin line from the outer corner of the eye towards the inner corner of the eye. Keep the tip of the eyeliner as close as possible to the lash line.

Pro Tip 1:

No transition shade? No worries! Your bronzer can double up as a perfect crease color. Multitasking at its finest!

Pro Tip 2:

Want your eye look to last from sunrise to sunset? Prime those lids with an eyeshadow primer first.

Pro Tip 3:

Use a waterproof eye pencil to give your line some extra staying power.

Pro Tip 4:

If you mess up, use a Q-tip to clean any part of your eyeliner that you want to correct. Just make sure you do it as soon as you mess up, before your eyeliner dries.

Eye Enchantment:

Let's talk eyes! What eyeshadow colors do you prefer for a simple, everyday look? Describe how you'd blend them together for that dreamy vibe.

Brow Basics:

Ah, the brows! They frame your face, so let's give 'em some love. Grab a brow pencil, lightly trace your natural shape, and fill in any sparse spots. Then, comb 'em upwards for that fluffy, natural look! Take a second look in the mirror, and go back and fill in any additional areas as needed to your taste.

Pro Tip 1:

Want more pronounced brows? Apply a bit more pressure with your pencil to make them a little darker. Easy peasy!

Pro Tip 2:

Keep those brows in check with regular grooming. A wax or threading sesh once a month keeps 'em looking sharp!

Brows That Wow:

Brows on fleek, always! How do you shape and fill in your brows for that natural yet defined look? Name one tip for creating the perfect arch.

Blushing Beauty:

Time to add a rosy glow! Blush is like a cherry on top of your makeup sundae. Dab a bit on the apples of your cheeks, then blend upwards towards your temples. Keep blending until you've got that "just ran a marathon but make it cute" vibe!

> **Pro Tip 1:**
> Feeling like you went a bit heavy-handed? No sweat! Dust a bit of powder over your blush to tone it down. Crisis averted!

Blush Bash:

Rosy cheeks, here we come! After applying blush, how do you blend it seamlessly into your skin? Describe the motion you'd use to diffuse the color.

Luscious Lips:

Finally, lips that speak volumes! Pick a lip color that matches your mood. Glossy, matte, sheer—it's your world, babe! Swipe it on, smack those lips together, and get ready to slay!

If you want your lips to look defined, use a lip liner close to the lip color of your choice to line your lips. Start at the top of the lips, feathering it to the corners of the mouth. Then, from the bottom, and feather towards the corner of the mouth.

Then apply the lipstick of your choice, and rub your lips together to blend it with the lipliner, and voila.

> **Pro Tip 1:**
> If you are a beginner, begin by choosing lip colors close to your natural lip color; they are more forgiving and are easier to fix in case you make a mistake. As you gain more experience and confidence in your application, experiment with different lipstick colors. You will be surprised as to how much fun you can have by changing them depending on your mood or occasion!

Lip color magic!

What's your lip color mood today: Glossy, matte, or something in between? Describe how you'd apply it for the perfect pout. Apply a little lip moisturizer or chapstick to prepare your lips for lip color.

NOTES

NOTES

NOTES

CHAPTER 3:
The Grand Finale

And there you have it, your masterpiece! Lock it all in with a spritz of setting spray. This baby will keep your glam on point from brunch to late-night shenanigans!

The Grand Finale: Setting Spray Showdown:

Lock it in, glam squad! Which setting spray do you choose to seal the deal? Write down one reason why setting spray is a must-have in your makeup routine.

Beauty Sleep:

Oh, and one last thing before you hit the hay! Always, always remove your makeup. Your skin needs to breathe, rejuvenate, and dream of even more fabulous makeup looks for tomorrow!

> **Pro Tip 1:**
> Use a good makeup remover, wash with a gentle cleanser, and show your skin some love with a night serum and moisturizer. Goodnight, glow-getter!

Nighttime Rituals:

Time to say goodnight to the glam! How do you remove your makeup at the end of the day? Describe your skincare routine before bedtime, from makeup remover to moisturizer.

NOTES

NOTES

NOTES

CHAPTER 4:

5-Minute Face

Mornings can be hectic, can't they? We've all been there - scrambling to get ready, running late, and wishing we had a little more time to finesse our makeup.

But have no fear, my friend! I've got your back with a quick and easy 5-minute makeup routine that'll have you looking perfectly polished, even on your busiest days.

Step 1: Skin Prep

Let's start by giving your complexion a quick boost. Smooth on a hydrating primer to create a smooth, even canvas. Follow up with a tinted moisturizer or lightweight, medium-coverage foundation - just enough to even out your skin tone without feeling cakey.

Quickly dab on a creamy concealer to cover any blemishes or dark circles, then set everything with a light dusting of translucent powder. This will help control shine and keep your makeup in place all day.

Step 2: Brows

Now let's move on to those brows! Use a tinted brow gel to quickly fill in and shape your arches. The built-in tint will add definition without looking too heavy-handed. Brush through with the spoolie to blend everything seamlessly.

Step 3: Eyes

For the eyes, reach for a neutral, matte eyeshadow palette. Sweep a warm, sandy shade all over the lid, then use a fluffy brush to diffuse a slightly deeper shade into the crease. This adds instant dimension without looking overdone.

Finish with a couple coats of lengthening black mascara, focusing on the tips of the lashes for a wide-awake, doe-eyed look.

Step 4: Cheeks

Time for a little pop of color! Smile and brush a peachy-pink powder blush onto the apples of your cheeks. Blend it up towards your temples for a healthy, youthful flush.

Step 5: Lips

Last but not least, moisturize your lips with a tinted lip balm or sheer lipstick. Go for a your-lips-but-better shade that'll complement the rest of your look.

And voila! You're done. The whole process should take you less than 5 minutes, leaving you with a polished, put-together look that's perfect for everyday wear.

Your Turn!

- What's your go-to quick makeup routine when you're short on time?
- Which step do you usually spend the most time on?
- Which areas of your face are most important to you?

NOTES

NOTES

CHAPTER 5:
Day to Night

Ah, the old "work to happy hour" dilemma - we've all been there! The key is to have a few go-to tricks up your sleeve to easily transform your makeup from office-ready to evening glam.

Day Look

When you're headed to the 9-to-5, you generally want a more low-key, natural makeup look. Think light, buildable coverage, subtle definition, and just a touch of color. The goal is polished perfection that still looks like you.

For the day, you might start with a luminous, medium-coverage foundation, just enough to even out your complexion. Follow up with a creamy concealer to camouflage any blemishes or dark circles. Set everything with a light dusting of translucent powder to blur pores and control shine.

On the eyes, use a neutral eyeshadow palette to create a soft wash of color on the lids. Define the lashline with a slim line of brown or taupe eyeliner, and finish with a coat or two of volumizing mascara. Fill in brows as needed to frame the face. (If you are in a rush, skip the eyeshadow.)

Lastly, a natural-looking rosy or coral blush on the apples of the cheeks, and a swipe of your favorite MLBB (my lips but better) lip color, and you're good to go!

Night Look

When the clock strikes 5 and it's time to transition to happy hour, you can take your look up a notch with just a few strategic tweaks.

Start by amping up the coverage with a fuller-coverage foundation. This will help create a more luminous, flawless canvas. Reach for a radiant concealer and dab it strategically under the eyes and on any problem areas.

For the eyes, reach for richer, more pigmented eyeshadows in shimmery or metallic finishes. Blend a warm, sultry brown into the crease, then pack on a shimmery champagne shade all over the lid. Use a gel or liquid liner to create a bold, dramatic wing. Finish with two coats of volumizing black mascara.

Take your bronzer and contour kit out of the drawer and use them to add some serious dimension to the face. Carefully sculpt the cheekbones, forehead, and jawline for a stunning, chiseled effect.

Finally, swap out that MLBB for a bold, long-wearing liquid lipstick in a rich, eye-catching shade. Pair it with a coordinating lip liner for extra definition and staying power.

Spritz on a setting spray to lock everything in place, and you're ready to take on the night! The transformation is complete.

Time to grab your friends and hit the town. Cheers!

Your Turn!

- What's your go-to quick makeup routine when you're short on time?
- Which step do you usually spend the most time on?
- Which areas of your face are most important to you?

NOTES

NOTES

CHAPTER 6:
Makeup Looks Decoded

Ah, the age-old makeup dilemma – what look should I go for today? Between soft glam, no-makeup makeup, and full-on glam, the options can feel overwhelming. But have no fear, I'm here to break down the key differences between some of the most popular makeup looks so you can figure out which one is right for you.

The "No Makeup" Makeup Look

This effortless, natural-looking style is all about enhancing your features while keeping things super low-key. The goal is to look like you're not wearing any makeup at all (even though you totally are).

The key elements :
- Lightweight, skin-perfecting foundation
- Just a touch of concealer where needed
- Subtle, natural-looking brows
- Neutral eyeshadows and a swipe of mascara
- A tinted lip balm or sheer lip color
- This look is great for everyday wear when you want to look polished but not overdone. It's all about that "your skin but better" vibe.

Soft Glam

Looking to take your makeup up a notch? Soft glam is the way to go. This look gives you a little more definition and drama, but still keeps things pretty and approachable.

The key elements :

- Medium to full coverage foundation
- Cream or powder contour to sculpt the face
- Warmer, more pigmented eyeshadows, often with a shimmer finish
- Fluttery lashes and a precision winged liner
- A creamy, long-wearing lip color
- Soft glam is perfect for special occasions, date nights, or anytime you want to look absolutely stunning. It's glam without feeling over-the-top.

Full Glam

And then there's the ultimate makeup look - full glam. This is for when you really want to make a statement and feel like a total show-stopper.

The key elements :
- High-coverage, luminous foundation
- Intense cream or powder contouring and highlighting
- Dramatic, jewel-toned eyeshadows, often paired with falsies
- Sharp, graphic eyeliner and bold, volumizing mascara
- A bold, high-impact lip, whether matte or glossy
- Full glam is all about turning up the drama and making a major impact. This look is perfect for special events, photo shoots, or anytime you want to feel like a total bombshell.

Your Turn!

- Which makeup look do you gravitate towards the most?
- What are some of the key differences you notice between these three looks?

NOTES

NOTES

NOTES

CHAPTER 7:
Skincare & Makeup Removal

Ahh, the often-overlooked but oh-so-important world of skincare. You know what they say - you can't have a flawless makeup look without a flawless canvas to start with! So let's dive in and talk all things skin.

Skincare Essentials

First thing's first – your daily skincare routine is the foundation (no pun intended) for healthy, glowing skin. Whether you have dry, oily, or combination skin, there are a few key steps you'll want to incorporate:

Cleanse: Start your day and end your night by gently washing your face with a mild, non-irritating cleanser. This helps remove dirt, oil, and any lingering makeup residue.

Tone: Follow up with a hydrating toner to rebalance your skin's pH and prep it for the next steps.

Treat: Whether it's a brightening serum, retinol treatment, or hydrating essence, be sure to incorporate a targeted skincare product to address your specific skin concerns.

Moisturize: Locking in moisture is key, so don't skip this crucial step! Find a moisturizer formulated for your skin type – bonus points if it has SPF for daytime use.

Mask: Once or twice a week, treat yourself to a nourishing face mask. This can help deeply cleanse, hydrate, or de-stress your skin.

The key is to listen to your skin and adjust your routine as needed. Consistency is key for seeing real results!

Makeup Removal

Okay, now that we've got the skincare basics down, let's talk about the not-so-fun part - taking off your makeup. I know, I know, sometimes it's tempting to just fall asleep with a full face still on. But trust me, your skin will thank you in the long run if you take the time to properly remove every last trace.

Start by using a micellar water or oil-based makeup remover to break down and lift away your foundation, concealer, and eye makeup. Gently sweep it over your face and eyes using a cotton pad or your fingertips.

Follow up with a gentle face wash to thoroughly cleanse away any remaining impurities. Be extra gentle around the delicate eye area.

Finally, use a toner to restore your skin's pH balance and prep it for the rest of your nighttime routine.

And don't forget - removing your makeup before bed allows your skin to breathe and regenerate while you sleep. It's a simple but essential step for maintaining a healthy, glowing complexion.

Your Turn!

- What's your current skincare routine looking like?
- How do you like to remove your makeup at the end of the day?

NOTES

NOTES

CHAPTER 8:
Skincare & Makeup Red Flags

Okay, let's talk about something super important when it comes to our beauty routines - knowing when a product might not be right for us. Because let's face it, not everything is going to work for every single person. Our skin and preferences are all unique, and it's important to pay attention to any red flags that pop up.

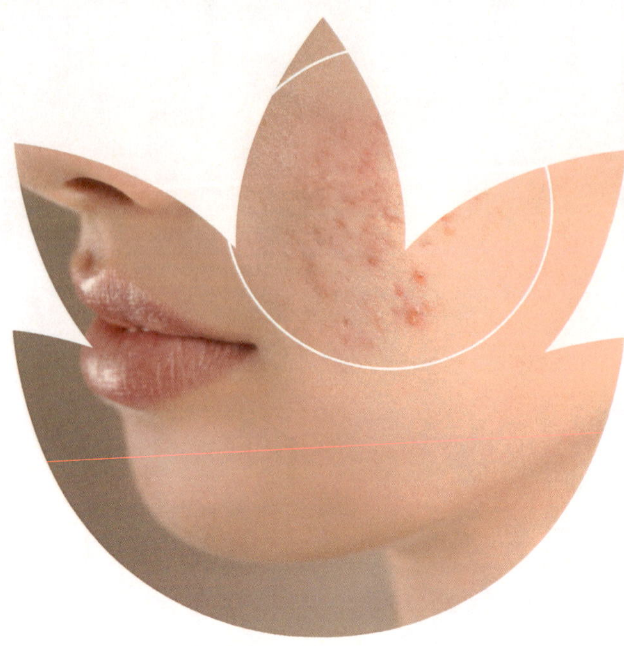

Red Flags for Skincare

So, how do you know if a skincare product isn't meshing well with your complexion? Here are some signs to look out for:

- **Irritation:** Did the product cause redness, stinging, or general discomfort when you applied it? That's a clear sign it might not be compatible with your skin.

- **Breakouts:** If you start noticing new blemishes or a general increase in congestion after using a product, it could be clogging your pores.

- **Dryness or Oiliness:** If your skin suddenly feels overly tight and dehydrated or excessively shiny and greasy, the formula might be throwing off your skin's natural balance.

- **Allergic Reaction:** In some cases, you may experience hives, swelling, or other visible allergic symptoms. If that happens, stop using the product immediately and consult a dermatologist.

Red Flags for Makeup

Makeup formulas can also cause issues if they don't quite mesh with your skin type or preferences. Watch out for these red flags:

- **Accentuated Texture:** If a foundation or concealer seems to be emphasizing the appearance of your pores, fine lines, or flaky patches, it might not be the right fit.

- **Separation or Pilling:** When a product starts to break down, pill up, or separate on the skin, that's a sure sign it's not playing nicely with the other products in your routine.

- **Irritation:** Just like with skincare, any stinging, redness, or general discomfort could indicate an allergic reaction or skin sensitivity.

- **Oxidation:** Have you ever noticed a foundation starting to look more orange or dull as the day wears on? That's oxidation, and it's a telltale sign the formula isn't quite right for you.

When to See a Dermatologist

If you're experiencing persistent issues with your skin or are just unsure about how to navigate all the options out there, it's always a good idea to consult a professional. A licensed dermatologist can help identify any underlying conditions, recommend tailored products and treatments, and give you personalized guidance on how to care for your unique complexion.

Don't be afraid to advocate for yourself and get the expert help you deserve! Your skin will thank you.

Your Turn!

- What are some red flags you've noticed with products in the past?
- Have you ever consulted a dermatologist about your skin concerns?
- How was that experience?

NOTES

NOTES

Bonus: Your Beauty Must-Haves

If you were stranded on a desert island and could only bring three makeup products, what would they be? Describe why these products are your go-to essentials.

Bonus 2: Share Your Makeup Journey

What's one makeup tip or trick you've learned that has changed your beauty game? Share it with us, and let's all level up our glam together!

BONUS
Brush Care Tips

The Fabulous Guide to Makeup Brush Care:

1. Get in the Habit of Regular Brush Baths:
- Why it's important: Think of it as giving your brushes a spa day! Regular cleaning keeps them fresh, happy, and free from makeup gunk that can lead to breakouts.

2. Treat Your Brushes to Gentle Cleansers:
- Why it's important: Harsh soaps are like drama queens—they cause unnecessary brush shedding! Stick to gentle cleansers that won't strip your brushes' personalities.

3. Rinse, Rinse, Baby:
- Why it's important: No one likes leftover soap residue—especially your skin! Rinse those babies under lukewarm water until they're squeaky clean.

4. Keep Water Away from the Ferrule (the Fancy Metal Part):
- Why it's important: Water and glue? Not a good mix! Avoid the drama of shedding by keeping water far away from the ferrule.

5. Shape Up Your Brushes:
- Why it's important: After their spa day, lay them flat on a towel to dry, and remind them they're fabulous just the way they are. No splaying allowed!

6. Dry Brush Drama:
- Why it's important: Nobody wants moldy brushes! Dry those beauties upside down to let them air out and avoid any unwanted mildew parties.

7. Give Them a Cozy Home:

- Why it's important: Brushes need their beauty sleep too! Store them upright in a clean, dry container or brush holder to keep them looking sharp.

8. Say No to Product Hoarding:

- Why it's important: Excessive product buildup? Ain't nobody got time for that! Tap off the excess before applying and give them a spa day regularly.

9. Cover Up for Protection:

- Why it's important: Just like how we wear hats in the sun, brushes need protection! Pop on some brush guards or covers to keep them safe and sound.

10. Keep Them Single and Ready to Mingle (with Makeup):

- Why it's important: Mixing products can lead to a makeup mishmash! Give each brush its own gig for powders, liquids, and creams to avoid a makeup party gone wrong.

11. Show Some TLC While Cleaning:

- Why it's important: Imagine cleaning brushes is like giving them a gentle massage—not a wrestling match! Treat them with love and they'll love you back.

12. Know When It's Time to Say Goodbye:

- Why it's important: Like old friends, brushes can't last forever. Replace them when they start acting out—shedding excessively or losing their shape.

> **Now you're ready to be the brush whisperer! With these tips, your brushes will be ready to create makeup magic every time you pick them up**

ABOUT ME

Ligia Centeno is a talented New England based Makeup Artist and owner of the successful company, Makeovers By Ligia. From simple and classic styles to bright, bold, and glamorous, Ligia works to create a look that is unique, timeless and meets all the needs of her clientele. She offers onsite makeup application services for brides throughout the New England area, with a focus on airbrush makeup applications. Her natural eye for beauty and specific attention to detail has brought her much success in the industry.

GET IN TOUCH

 info@makeoversbyligia.com

 www.makeoversbyligia.com